this reminded me of *forever*

Bella Karad

COMPLETE YOUR *"YOU, US, FOREVER"* COLLECTION

Copyright ©2025 Bella Karad

All rights reserved.

No portion of this book may be reproduced in any form without written permission from the publisher or author, except as permitted by U.S. copyright law.

ISBN: 9798282236941

This Reminded Me of Forever *Bella Karad*

Dedicated to *you,*
 us,
 forever.

They say soulmates recognize each other instantly, and I think that's why I felt so comfortable with you from the very start. There was no hesitation, no awkwardness, just a quiet certainty that you belonged in my life.

I didn't need time to realize how much you meant to me. Every laugh we shared, every glance, every little moment.

My heart always knew.

You're not just my person,
you're my forever.

You will always have
a special place in my heart.

A place that you created,
a place nobody else can take.

Talk to date.

Date to marry.

Marry to grow old together.

Only way it should be.

I used to think my love language was physical touch, but I've realized it's words of affirmation.

When someone explains in detail how they feel about me, being told the little things that they think makes me special, the constant reassurance... I love hearing how much I'm loved.

You give me all this.

You're my first.

And I don't mean my first kiss,
  or my first relationship,
  or my first I love you.

You're the first person
  who makes me feel like I'm enough
  and the first one to show me
  what I love you actually means.

From my book "Starlit Dreams"

As long as I'm still breathing,
you will always have someone
who is proud of you in everything.

I don't want a perfect relationship.

I just want us to never give up on each other.

I may make mistakes.
But loving you was never a mistake.

Despite all of my faults,
I will always try to be better for you,
because I don't want to lose you,
because you deserve the best,
   and I want to be the one to give that to you.

I love you,
and I want to have you by my side for the rest of my life,
   because for me, you're more than enough.

Proud of you today,
  proud of you tomorrow,
    proud of you forever,

because you are one of the strongest people I know.

Your first love isn't always the first person
you kissed or the first person you dated.

Your first love is the person
you will always compare everyone to.

I never believed in happy endings,
because they never really seemed to exist.

   Not until I met you
and you made me believe.

   I couldn't resist,
resist you and me.

   We were so impossible
never did I know,
I'd love you with all my heart
   and you'd love me too

   But now that we do,
I can delightedly say
that you are my life
   and not just a part.

From my book "Golden Moonlight"

No matter what you think about yourself,

in my eyes,

you are always perfect.

Thank you for making me feel
　loved,
　　special,
　　　and cared for.

Thank you for giving me
　the love I never got,
　　and loving me the way
　　　that I am.

Thank you for everything
　that you've done for me.

And thank you
　for coming into my life.

Thank you
for being the kindest
and dearest person
in my life.

I love you,
and I will keep reminding you of that
forever.

To be loved like a habit,
    not a chore.

To be loved like a breath,
    not a sigh.

To be loved like a song,
    not a noise.

To be loved like a privilege,
    not an obligation.

My love,
I can think of so many
things to say to you,
but when I see you,
I get tongue-tied.

And if I say what I'm thinking,
it will never come out
the way I want it to.

That's what you do to me;
you affect me with your existence.

I'm sitting here,
the thought itself
is sickening;
How I love the way
you make me feel
so much.

But all I do is hear you speak,
hoping that one day,
I can tell you
how much you mean to me.

That, my darling,
you any more than words
will ever be.

From my book "Starlit Dreams"

> Everything happens for a reason.

For example:
> you and I met
>> because we're going to get married.

Learning to control my overthinking,
> because I want to be with you.

Learning to not self-sabotage,
> because I want to be with you.

Learning to control my anger,
> because I want to be with you.

Learning to not go quiet when I'm upset,
> because I want to be with you.

Learning to be a better person,
> so I can make things work,
>> because I finally feel loved,
>>> and really want to be with you.

I would still kiss you when you're sick,
knowing I would get sick too.

I would never stop loving you,
even if you stop loving me.

I would sit and hold you for hours,
just to be a little closer to you.

I would check up on you a hundred times,
just to make sure you're okay..

I will always be there for you,
   no matter what happens.

"Even at my worst?"
                Even at your worst.

"Even when I'm mad at you?"
                Even when you're mad at me.

"Even when I make a mistake?"
                Even when you make a mistake.

"Even when I'm crying?"
                Even when you're crying.

"Even when I'm happy?"
                Even when you're happy.

                I love you no matter the situation.

I didn't fall in love with you at first glance.
  My love for you grew slowly, with time.

It was the way you held my hand,
  the way you looked at me
  from across the room,
  the way your eyes lit up
  when you smiled at me,
  the way your scent stayed
  on my clothes for days;
  the way you made me
  feel safe in your presence.

I didn't fall in love with you at first glance.
  I fell in love with the way you loved me.

From my book "Starlit Dreams"

I know it's been hard for both of us lately,
but I hope you won't get tired of us.

For all the fights and the boring days
I hope you'll still choose to stay with me.

We are in a relationship at this young age,
  and I don't expect it to be perfect.

No, we're not toxic,
  we are simply two kids,
  trying our best to love each other.

Please don't give up on me.

I'm not the easiest to love,
  but I love you with all I have.

As
long
as
I'm
with
you,

I've
got
a
smile
on
my
face.

Proud of you today.
    Proud of you tomorrow.
        Proud of you every day.

Because you are
one of the strongest people
that I know.

You are the most gentle,
caring person I've ever known.

From the moment I met you,
I felt like I had finally
found where I belong,
as if we were always meant
to cross paths, to be a part
of each other's story.

Never did I imagine that,
out of billions of people,
there would be someone
as extraordinary as you,
a soul so perfectly
aligned with mine.

I don't say it enough,
but I truly believe
you were brought
into my life
to be my sanctuary,
my peace,
and my heart's
true home.

From my book "Golden Moonlight"

I want to work on myself
with you by my side.

I want you to work on yourself
with me by yours.

Life is not easy.
Let's do this together.

Unfortunately,
me and you have to get married.

Because there's no way I'm letting
someone else's child have the same eyes
I fell in love with.

With or without me,
I want you to see you live your life happily.

Together or not together,
I hope the universe takes care of you
no matter what.

I'll never forget the night that I noticed.

We were both so in love.

I may not be perfect,
but really love you with all my heart.

I like the way we feel together.

We fit.

To you:

I love you.

And I will do everything I can to make us work. Because I want a future with you, to spend my life with you, to grow old with you. Because you are the only person I want to be with.

So,

will you step on the boat
and sail in the sea
in this adventure
with me?

From my book "Starlit Dreams"

I

hope

you

stay

in

my

life

forever.

I'm sorry for all my mistakes.

I'm trying to be better for you,
   but I'm scared of losing you,
   and I just want you
   to stay in my life.

I'm so sorry if my actions
   have ever made you feel
   unwanted by me,

   because I care.

I just don't always know
   how to show it.

I am yours.

                You are mine.

And I promise to love you truly
  and unconditionally,
and to stand by your side
  no matter what.

Me

&

you.

Forever.

Okay?

Happiness
is just part of our journey.

> Unconditional love,
> > undying commitment,
> > > will make it last.

From my book "Bottled Feelings"

You are,
without a doubt,
the love of my life.

Just wanna hold you
and not let go for hours.

The day I met you
I started to forget
my life without you.

And when it's late at night,
and the world is quiet,
I think of you.

I'm still looking for a phrase
　stronger than *I love you*.

You don't deserve a paragraph.

　　You deserve a thousand books
　written about how wonderful you are.

　I can't wait for the day
when I don't have to say good night
　through the phone,

　　but instead do it
　looking into your eyes.

Many boys will bring you flowers.

But one day,
  you will meet a boy,
    who will learn
your favorite flower,
  your favorite scent,
    your favorite sweet.

  And it won't matter if
he can't give you many of them,
because he will have taken the time
to know you,

  as no one else has done.

      Only that boy
    deserves your heart.

I'm convinced that
I was made to love you.

                        If you aren't busy
                        for the next 70 years,

I would love to
spend them with you.

                        I will choose you
                        time and *time again*.

In your eyes
  I wanna drown.

    In your lips
      I wanna melt.

        In your warmth
          I wanna die.

            And in your arms
              I wanna be buried.

From my book "Golden Moonlight"

To be honest,
you're more than just my favorite person.

You're different from everyone.

You have a special place
in my heart.

You are more loved than you know,

> more valuable than you realize.

> more capable than you believe.

> more important than you understand.

Falling for you was
the most unplanned thing in my life,
  and it turned out to be
the best thing that's ever happened.

  Being away from you
is the greatest reminder
  of how much your presence
means to me.

  I love you,
I will keep loving you
  until I die.

   And if there's life after that,
    I will love you then, too.

The

first

thing

that

pops

into

my

mind

every

morning

is

you.

I thought I knew what love meant.
I tried so hard not to fall for you,
because I thought that to love
  was just another way to get hurt.

But you taught me that love
doesn't have to be that way.
Because loving you feels safe.
It feels fuzzy and warm.
  It feels like home.

From my book "Starlit Dreams"

Run to me
>   when the world gets mean to you, okay?

Talk to me
>   when everything is overwhelming, okay?

Hold my hand
>   when you feel like you have no one, okay?

You will
>   always have me right next to you, okay?

I always want to kiss you.

Even the second we pull away,
I want to kiss you again.

My heart belongs to you,
and only you.

Forever
choosing
you.

Don't ever give up on something
you can't go a day without thinking about.

  If it makes you happy,
then it's not a waste of time.

  Everything will be okay in the end.

  If it's not okay,
then it's not the end.

It doesn't need to make sense to other people.

When you fall in love with a pair of eyes,
you become blind to all other eyes.

You make me feel beautiful
in these three little ways:

by holding my hands,
  looking me in the eyes,
    and calling me yours.

From my book "Golden Moonlight"

I hope you know

that I only have eyes for you,

that you brought my spark back,

that I really do love you,

that in you I see my future.

I will never love another soul

the way I love yours.

I have never met a soul who
　could speak my language,
　until there was you.

You are fluent in me.

　You feel more like home
　than any place I've been.

I've never been good
　at telling people how I feel,
　but you made me want to try.

I'm too late to be your first love,
but I'll do anything to be your last.

I can't promise to solve all your problems,
but what I can promise is you won't have to
face them alone.

I want nothing more than to have you
for the rest of my life.

I didn't fall for you
because I was chasing a fairytale,
or because my life felt incomplete,
or just to feel less lonely.

I fell for you
because your smile feels like
a warm welcome into a loving home.

Then I fell for you
because being around you feels like
peace in all the chaos.

And then I fell for you
because loving you feels like breathing;
natural and necessary.

And the simplest reason
why I keep falling for you
is because you are you.

From my book "Golden Moonlight"

I will love you until the world fades away,

and if something awaits us beyond this life,

my love will find you there too.

This Reminded Me of Forever

Bella Karad

I didn't know what love was
  when I first fell for you.

I stayed because you made me feel
  something no one else ever could.

And I keep falling, day after day,
  because I can't see my future
    with anyone but you.

My goal is to marry you,
  build with you,
    grow with you.

I see everything
  in you
    and
      in us.

My

heart

was

made

to

love

yours.

When my cheeks kept hurting from smiling,
    my heart kept fluttering,
    my legs felt weak,
    and eye contact with you
    became my favorite thing,

        that's when I realized:

the longer I stare at you,
the more beautiful you become;
    silky hair,
    sparkling eyes,
    soothing voice,
    soft lips,
    kindest heart.

        You're mesmerizing.

From my book "Golden Moonlight"

I know that people come and go,
but I hope we stay until we grow old.

I don't think you understand
how beautiful you make my world
just be existing in it.

I hope you know I will always
clap the loudest for you.

This Reminded Me of Forever *Bella Karad*

You could show me the parts of yourself
that you think are too damaged to share,
the parts you've kept hidden because
you're afraid no one would understand,
 and even then I wouldn't turn away.

I would look at you and still see
everything that makes you *you*.
None of it would scare me;
 I will always see you shining.

In the end,
we will be together.

No matter the distance
or the time it takes.

We will be together.

I promised you.

I will never leave you
no matter what life throws at us.

I will never get tired of loving you,
because loving you is my happiness.

I promised you.

This Reminded Me of Forever

Bella Karad

I don't think anyone loves
  the way that I do,
I don't think anyone can love you
  the way that I love you.

  I know they don't,
and no matter what you do,
  I won't stop loving you,
the way just I do.

From my book "Golden Moonlight"

My dream?

You.

Us.

Forever.

If I had to do life all over again,
  I would find you sooner,
    so I can love you longer.

My soul was made to love yours.

I

don't

want

this

night

to

ever

end.

You are my favorite person,

and I will love you

always

& forever.

This Reminded Me of Forever   *Bella Karad*

There is art
in your heart,
painting pictures,
when I lay my head
down on your chest.

There are songs
in your eyes,
singing lullabies,
when you hover
pinning me down
with your stare.

There is a poem
on the tip of your tongue;
I taste it
when I kiss you.

From my book "Bottled Feelings"

I believe in forever
only if it's with you.

I don't love you
　with my heart
　or my mind.

I love you
　with my soul.

In case my mind forgets
　and my heart stops.

We talk about getting married
and having babies so casually.

And I'm trying not to cry
because little me never thought
I would be loved like this.

Falling for you was
the most unplanned thing,
and you turned out to be
the love of my life.

Falling in love with you
  wasn't a quick spark
  or a sudden rush.

It was the way you listened,
like every word I said mattered.

The way your laughter felt like sunlight;
  and your touch felt like home;
  and your presence felt like a hug.

And how you never asked me
to be anyone but myself.

It wasn't one moment;
  it was every small, gentle thing
  you did without even knowing.

From my book "Golden Moonlight"

Two

souls

don't

meet

by

accident.

Little me

always dreamed

of having

someone *like you*.

When I say *I love you*,

I mean *I want you in my life forever.*

You healed pieces of me
I didn't know needed healing.

You cared for me
when I didn't know
I could use
that extra love.

You brought out
the happiness in me
I didn't know existed.

You've made me feel
more alive than ever.

Be mine forever.

From my book "Starlit Dreams"

You're

my

softest

and

silliest

dream

by the way.

Show me where it hurts,

  so I know where to love you

    the most.

Finally,
I found my happiness,

and it's you.

From my book "Starlit Dreams"

Your eyes didn't just look at me.

They *saw* me.

When you tell me I'm beautiful,

    you don't realize you're the first one

        to actually make me believe it.

You touched my heart so softly
when everything around me was cruel.

I had no option but to fall for you completely.

Bella Karad

  Being with you
feels like stillness
without emptiness.

  Just peace,
soft and steady.

From my book "Golden Moonlight"

You are dancing in my heart
to the secret song of my soul.

I want you.

   All of you.

Your flaws,
your mistakes,
your imperfections.

   I want *all* of you.

Love is giving someone
the power to destroy you,
and trusting they won't use it.

Let's take pictures.

Not together,
but of each other.

  So when you look at the picture
you remember the moment,
not because you see me there,
but because you relive the moment
  all over again.

From my book "Starlit Dreams"

You make me feel softer,
yet somehow, even the hardest days
feel lighter when you're near.

This Reminded Me of Forever

Bella Karad

I don't love you just for who you are today,
   but for every quiet moment we've shared,
   every laugh that made time stop,
   and every day still waiting for us.

You're not just part of my life,
   you've become the place where
   my heart belongs,

and I want every tomorrow
   with you in it.

Every version of the future I want

has you in it.

Not as an option,

but as the constant.

I know what I want.

I want you in the morning,
  pouring your coffee
  after a morning kiss.

I want you in the nighttime,
  when you're tired from the day,
  but still want to spend the rest with me.

I want to gaze at you
  like the masterpiece you are.

   I want to be the one for you.

There,

under barely any light,

I find art within your eyes,

as like stars are found in the night's sky,

you're a masterpiece no darkness can hide.

From my book "Golden Moonlight"

This Reminded Me of Forever

Bella Karad

You're in every hope I have,
  every dream I chase,
and every tomorrow I imagine.

No matter how much time passes
  or how the world changes,
my heart will always belong to you.

I don't just love who you are now,

I love every version of you I have yet to meet.

Thank you for reading
this reminded me of *forever*

I love you.

COMPLETE YOUR *"YOU, US, FOREVER"* COLLECTION

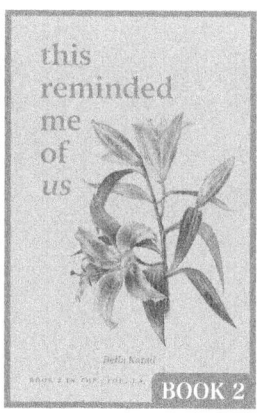

EXPLORE THE *"STARLIT DREAMS"* COLLECTION

Printed in Dunstable, United Kingdom